A *fashionable* HISTORY of COATS & TROUSERS

A FASHIONABLE HISTORY OF COATS &
TROUSERS
was produced by

David West 🕴 **Children's Books**
7 Princeton Court
55 Felsham Road
London SW15 1AZ

Author: Helen Reynolds
Editor: Clare Hibbert
Picture Research: Carlotta Cooper
Designer: Julie Joubinaux

First published in Great Britain in 2003 by
Heinemann Library, Halley Court, Jordan Hill,
Oxford OX2 8EJ, a division of
Harcourt Education Ltd.

OXFORD MELBOURNE AUCKLAND
JOHANNESBURG BLANTYRE GABORONE
IBADAN PORTSMOUTH (NH) USA CHICAGO

07 06 05 04 03
10 9 8 7 6 5 4 3 2 1

ISBN 0 431 18334 1 (HB)
ISBN 0 431 18342 2 (PB)

British Library Cataloguing in Publication Data

Reynolds, Helen
A fashionable history of coats and trousers
1. Coats - History - Juvenile literature 2. Pants -
History - Juvenile literature 3. Fashion - History
- Juvenile literature
I. Title II. Coats and trousers
391'.009

Printed and bound in China

PHOTO CREDITS :
Abbreviations: t-top, m-middle, b-bottom, r-right,
l-left, c-centre.

Front cover m & 16-17t, tl & 16bm, r & 10r –
Mary Evans Picture Library.
Pages 3 & 8-9, 4tr & 6tl, 6bl & r, 8tl, 10l & tm,
11tl & tr, 12l, tm & r, 16l, 18bl, 18-19, 19tr & l,
20tl & bl, 26tl & r – Mary Evans Picture Library.
16-17t – Mary Evans/Lesley Bradshaw Collection.
4br, 7tr & bl, 8bl, 11bl, 14m, 22l, 22tr – Dover
Books. 4-5b, 15br, 27br, 28br, 29tr – Corbis
Images. 5tr, 24tr – The Culture Archive. 5br, 11br,
13ml & tr, 15tr & bl, 17bl, 19br, 21 all, 22br,
23 all, 25tr & bl, 27l – Rex Features Ltd. 7br –
Digital Stock. 7tl – The Kobal Collection/20th
Century Fox. 9tr – The Kobal Collection/Scott
Free/Enigma/Paramount. 17tr – The Kobal
Collection/Paramount. 24bl – The Kobal
Collection/Warner Bros. 26bl – The Kobal
Collection/Associated British. 12bm – Karen
Augusta, www.antique-fashion.com. 14l –
© National Trust Photographic Library/John
Hammond. 18br – © National Trust
Photographic Library/Andreas von Einsiedel. 20-
21m – © National Trust Photographic Library.

Every effort has been made to contact copyright
holders of any material reproduced in this book.
Any omissions will be rectified in subsequent
printings if notice is given to the publishers.

*An explanation of difficult words can be
found in the glossary on page 31.*

A fashionable HISTORY *of* COATS & TROUSERS

Heinemann
LIBRARY

Contents

SAXON MANTLE

This Saxon king is wearing a mantle – a loose-fitting cloak that wrapped around the shoulders for warmth.

TARTAN SUIT

The traditional suit is a pair of trousers with matching jacket. This one is made from tartan, a popular, checked fabric made from woven wool.

From capes to combats

IN THEIR SIMPLEST FORM *trousers and coats can be traced back to the loincloth and to the T-shaped tunic worn as outerwear. Refined by different cultures over time, these basic garments are still recognizable in many areas of the world including India and the Middle East. In the West, clothing similar to modern trousers and coats first appeared in the 17th century. In the 18th and 19th centuries, advances in tailoring techniques further refined these garments.*

Today, with so many fabrics and styles, coats and trousers can be very simple – or extremely complex.

JEANS

Once worn only as workwear, over the last five decades jeans have become the most popular leisure trouser.

MODERN MATERIALS

This ski suit is made from Gore-Tex™, a man-made fabric designed for sports clothes that is super-warm, but also allows the skin to breathe. For high visibility, this suit also has reflective, yellow panels.

CAMOUFLAGE COMBATS

Originally designed for soldiers in the army, multi-pocketed baggy combats are now fashionable for both sexes.

From cloak to cape

Kingly cloak

This Saxon monarch's scarlet mantle is a simply-cut piece of cloth, pinned together on the left shoulder (CE 850s).

COSTUME de COUR 1588

Short & showy

Renaissance cloaks were worn indoors as well as out. They were decorative, rather than warm.

THE FIRST CLOAKS WERE SIMPLE PIECES OF CLOTH *that wrapped around the body. Cloaks, in one form or another, were worn by the earliest civilizations. Loose cloaks remained the main outer garment until the Middle Ages. After that, the cloak was shaped to fit more snugly over the shoulders, arms and body.*

Ornate copes & capes

Medieval men and women wore a semicircular cope – a sleeveless form of cape. This garment was also adopted by the clergy. Ecclesiastical copes were lavishly embroidered with precious threads in silks, silver and gold. Even today, many cathedrals still have a cope chest, where they store these clothes.

In the Renaissance short, embroidered capes were very fashionable for men. But from the 1700s, men began to wear coats rather than capes.

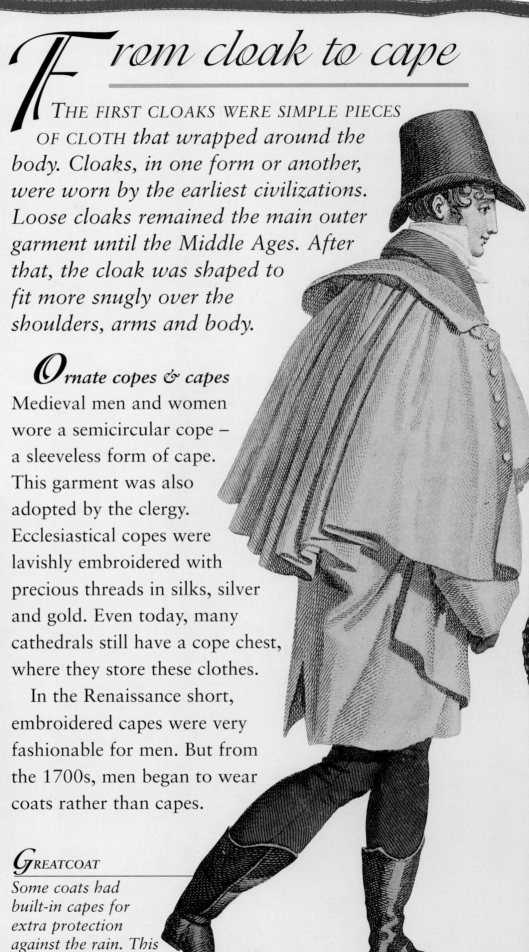

Greatcoat

Some coats had built-in capes for extra protection against the rain. This one is from 1810.

Women's capes & cloaks

Women carried on wearing cloaks until the 20th century. They switched to coats as their clothes became more fitted. Then, in the 1950s, there was a brief fashion for capes as evening wear. French couturier Pierre Balmain (1914–82) designed Russian-style capes while, in the United States, Pauline Trigère (1912–2002) introduced soft, woollen capes.

Ethnic and traditional capes, such as ponchos, became fashionable with hippies in the late 1960s. The look was revived in the early 21st century.

Sherlock Holmes

The caped greatcoat is often known as a 'Sherlock Holmes coat'. The fictional detective wore a tweed one, with a matching deerstalker hat.

Opera-cloak

Men's capes were popular evening wear in the 1800s. Opera-cloaks were worn over full evening dress.

Outsize outerwear

In the 1800s, women wore hooded cloaks or lacy shawls. Outer garments needed to be amply sized – to fit over the enormous skirts.

Traditional South American ponchos

The poncho, from South America, is a form of cape. It is a simple rectangle of fabric, with a hole cut for the head.

Doublets to bomber jackets

DOUBLETS WERE FIRST WORN BY MEN *in the 1300s.*
They were close-fitting, waisted jackets with detachable sleeves.
From the 1400s, doublets were padded with wool or horsehair.
Padding kept the wearer warm – and also gave him a macho
physique! Doublets were often slashed, so that the shirt
underneath poked through. They remained popular until
the 1600s.

Peasecods

Around 1575,
peasecod-bellied
doublets came
into fashion. They
had extra padding
at the front –
so the wearer
seemed to have
a pot-belly!

Knightly attire

These knights of the 1440s
wore doublets. The padding
offered some protection
against enemy arrows.

Waistcoats

From the 1500s, gentlemen wore sleeveless jackets,
called jerkins. By the 1700s a sleeveless undercoat, later
to be called a waistcoat, was also
popular. It reached the knee, but
soon shortened. Men left their
coats unbuttoned to show off
their dazzling waistcoats. Even in
the 1800s, when men's clothes became
rather sombre, waistcoats remained
fancy – although they now
matched the trousers or jacket.

Women's waistcoats

Gypsy waistcoats were
part of traditional
women's dress, especially
in areas of Eastern
Europe. In the late
1800s, working women
began to wear masculine
waistcoats with the new,
jacket-and-skirt suits.

8

ARTILLERY JACKET

The short jackets worn by 19th-century hussars were tight-fitting. In the 20th century, military jackets were cut more generously. They also came in colours such as khaki – that gave far better camouflage!

Styles for soldiers... & civvies

Until around 1900, military jackets were modelled on the doublet, but their close fit hampered movement. By World War I (1914–18), roomier, hip-length battle jackets were worn instead. New jackets developed for those fighting in World War II (1939–45) included the Eisenhower and bomber jackets, both of which came in wool or leather.

The Eisenhower jacket was named after Dwight Eisenhower (1890–1969), Supreme Commander of Allied forces. It had stylish epaulettes (shoulder straps) and stopped at the waist with a buttoned belt.

The bomber jacket was worn by pilots. It had an elasticated waist and zipped up at the front. Both these styles were adapted for civilian wear after the war – and they are still popular today.

BOMBER JACKET

Now widely worn as casual wear, bomber jackets were first designed for fighter pilots in World War II.

Breeches & plus-fours

BREECHES DEVELOPED FROM THE TRUNK-HOSE *worn in the 16th century. These consisted of puffed-out trunks that came to mid-thigh, and stockings (hose) that covered the rest of the leg.*

By the 17th century, trunks had lengthened to become breeches. Men wore breeches until around 1850, though at the end they were only a court fashion.

Nobleman

This gentleman of 1789 wears striped silk stockings and slimline, gold breeches. Braces under the frock-coat hold up the breeches.

Venetians

Both trunk-hose and breeches were worn in the late 16th century. These men wear Venetians, a style of breeches.

The 1600s

Full, knickerbocker-style breeches had strings that tied at the back of the waist. Then, in the late 1600s, braces were introduced. The new invention meant that breeches could be narrower, and have a looser waistband.

Petticoat breeches

These petticoat breeches of 1630 originated in France. The full leg looked like a skirt or petticoat – especially if trimmed with frilly lace!

Breeches come back!

By the 1920s, men wanted more comfortable styles, especially for sports. They adopted plus-fours, which were like breeches, only longer and fuller. Their name referred to the extra four inches (10 cm) of cloth beneath the knee. The Prince of Wales (1894–1972) made plus-fours popular after wearing them to play golf. The knickerbocker look was revived in the 1970s, only this time for women rather than men.

PLUS-FOURS

In the 1920s, tweed plus-fours were often teamed with a patterned Fair Isle sweater and matching socks.

CASUAL CLOTHES IN THE UNITED STATES

This young American gent of 1927 has the relaxed and easy look of knickerbockers, sports jacket and tie, and a button-up waistcoat.

BREECHES FOR SPORTS

Breeches were part of the usual uniform for 19th-century sportsmen. This man is playing American baseball.

SPANISH BULLFIGHTER IN BREECHES

Today, bullfighters still wear colourful brocade breeches in the bullring. A matching jacket and scarlet cape complete the look.

Trousers

In the 1800s long trousers began to replace breeches for everyday wear. They were held up with braces and had stirrup-style straps that went under the shoe to stop them riding up. Fly fronts – with buttons, not zips – first appeared in 1823. They became widespread in the 1840s, about the same time that trousers became straighter.

Saxon trousers

This Anglo-Saxon wore woollen stockings and leg bandages. He would have worn braies beneath his tunic.

Neat creases

Trousers were always pressed with the crease at the side, along the seam. Front-creased trousers only came into fashion in the early 1900s, after the invention of the trouser press.

Dandy

These trousers of 1826 were cut generously over the hip and thigh, then skin-tight below the knee.

Fancy braces

Braces are straps that hold up the trousers. These floral ones are from the 1800s.

Russian style

Trousers based on those worn by the Russian cavalry were fashionable in the early 1800s. Cossack trousers had a pleated waist and narrow legs.

Trousers for young followers of fashion

The 1950s saw the birth of youth fashions. With more spending money than ever before, young people no longer dressed just like their parents. The mod, or modernist, look of the early 1960s was all about being snappily dressed – and that meant dark suits with short jackets and tight, drainpipe trousers.

In the late 1960s a completely new trouser style emerged, that appealed to both men and women. Cut low and tight around the hips, these trousers flared out from the thighs. Flares came back into fashion in the late 1990s.

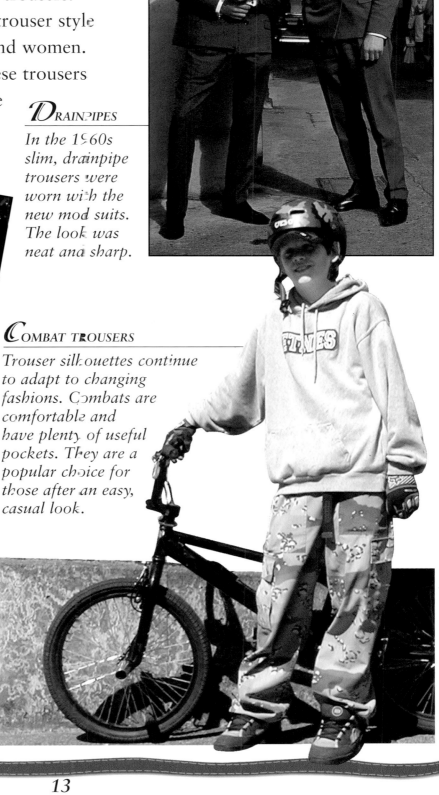

Drainpipes

In the 1960s slim, drainpipe trousers were worn with the new mod suits. The look was neat and sharp.

Combat trousers

Trouser silhouettes continue to adapt to changing fashions. Combats are comfortable and have plenty of useful pockets. They are a popular choice for those after an easy, casual look.

Flares hit the dance floor

Flares were fashionable in the 1970s. John Travolta (b.1954) famously danced in a flared suit in the film Saturday Night Fever *(1974).*

Baggy trousers

POPULAR IN THE MIDDLE EAST FOR CENTURIES, *baggy trousers were not widely worn in the West until the 20th century. Except for braies, which were an early form of drawers, modern long trousers did not appear until the 1800s.*

Where to stop?

Most long trousers stop at the ankle. Not so with those in this Samurai-style costume – or with 21st-century teenagers!

Wide boys

The 19th-century fashion for slim-fitting trousers lasted until the early 1920s. Then, trousers were cut with a wider leg and turn-ups were added to the hem. This fashion was taken to extremes by some students at Oxford University. They wore baggy trousers that measured 50 cm across at the bottom hem. Before long, wide trousers like these were nicknamed Oxford bags. The style was adopted by young women in the 1930s and 1970s.

Styles for a traveller

Thomas Legh (1792–1857) explored the Nile in 1812. He wore baggy, North African pants for this portrait, rather than the slim fashions of the day.

Fashions from America

Wide trousers for men remained popular thoughout the 1930s, thanks to the relaxed tailoring worn by Hollywood stars such as Clark Gable (1901–60) and Humphrey Bogart (1899–1957). Around this time, belts replaced braces. Belted trousers sat lower on the hip, so they looked even baggier.

In the 1940s and 1950s, there was a craze among Americans of Mexican or African origin for zoot suits. These had extremely baggy trousers that tapered in at the bottom. The style never really caught on in Europe, where fabrics were still in short supply after the war.

Zoot suit

The zoot suit used lots of fabric for its full, baggy trousers and wide-shouldered jacket. The style was popular with jazz musicians, such as Cab Calloway (1907–94), shown right.

Gangster chic

Soccer star Ian Wright (b.1963) poses in a modern-day gangster suit. In the 1930s, Chicago gangsters were known for their trademark baggy suits and trilby hats.

Baggy boarder

In the 1990s, outsize baggy trousers were all the rage with skateboarders and rappers. The look originated in New York but soon spread across the world.

In her newspaper, The Lily, Amelia Bloomer called on all sensible women to adopt this outfit.

Women in trousers

IN THE EARLY 1850S, THE AMERICAN ELIZABETH SMITH MILLER (1822–1911) *noticed women in Swiss health sanatoriums wore Turkish trousers under short, loose dresses. She decided to adopt the same outfit, encouraging her cousin, Elizabeth Cady Stanton (1815–1902), and Amelia Bloomer (1818–94) to do the same. The bloomer outfit was born.*

The short-lived fashion for bloomers

Worn without a corset, the bloomer outfit was comfortable as well as practical. It was very popular with early feminists. Unfortunately, they were widely ridiculed. By 1860 the outfit was dropped, so that women's rights campaigners would be taken seriously.

TROUSER SUIT OF 1919

After World War I, it became more acceptable for women to wear trousers.

DRESSED FOR CYCLING

The bicycle, photographed here in 1896, was a new and popular invention. Cycling was difficult in a full skirt, so divided skirts were designed.

SLACKS FOR BEATNIKS

Actress Audrey Hepburn (1928–93) starred as a beatnik (bohemian) in Funny Face (1957). By the 1950s, well-cut trousers were part of every fashionable young woman's wardrobe. It took another decade for trousers to be worn by older women.

FORTIES TROUSER SUITS

In the early 1940s, many women signed up for war work away from home. Freer than ever before, some adapted masculine trousers, shirts and jackets for everyday wear.

DUNGAREES

Dungarees were originally worn by working men. In World War II, they were worn by women working in factories, producing arms and other vital supplies.

Pushing for change

During the 1880s, the newly-formed Rational Dress Society promoted a bifurcated garment, that is, a divided skirt or culottes. This became popular with lady cyclists, but was not accepted by the public at large. In one famous court case, a judge ruled that it was right that a lady in a bifurcated garment had been thrown out of a hotel!

World War I changed all this. Taking over men's jobs, women also began to wear masculine trousers for both work and leisure. In World War II, land girls (farm hands) and factory workers routinely wore them. Today trousers are a key part of women's dress.

Dress-coats

DRESS-, OR FROCK-COATS ARE TIGHT-FITTING, FORMAL COATS *that have tails at the back and a cutaway or square front. First worn in the late 18th century, they evolved into modern morning coats (worn in the day) and dinner jackets (for evening).*

Frocks to show off in

In the late 18th century, the full-skirted frock-coats worn for riding were adapted in finer fabrics. Popular in the royal courts of Europe, these lavishly-embroidered frock-coats were unbuttoned to display colourful waistcoats. Around 1800, fashionable frock-coats were double-breasted and worn with a large cravat. By 1850, they were plain and dark, though some had shiny, satin lapels.

Day coat

With a cutaway front and broad, square tails, this frock-coat of 1829 is typical of the time. It is worn with instep trousers, square-toed shoes and a top hat.

Velvet frock-coat

This maroon frock-coat of 1770 had a matching waistcoat and breeches. Silk stockings covered the legs.

Napoleonic style

After the Revolution (1789) frock-coats in France were less showy – but the clothes underneath were not!

Tuxedos for men... & women

In the 1880s a tail-less black jacket, called a dinner jacket, became popular for less formal occasions. In the United States it was named the tuxedo, after the Tuxedo Club in New Jersey.

In 1966 Yves Saint Laurent (*b*.1936) introduced tuxedo suits as evening wear for women. These remained popular up until the 1980s.

WALKING COAT

Also of 1829, this variation of the frock-coat does not cut away at the front, but is one length all the way round.

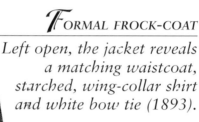

FORMAL FROCK-COAT

Left open, the jacket reveals a matching waistcoat, starched, wing-collar shirt and white bow tie (1893).

MORNING COAT

In the early 20th century, morning coats were worn to the office. Today, they are reserved for formal occasions.

DINNER JACKETS TODAY

Worn with a white shirt and black tie, it's easy to see why DJs are nicknamed 'penguin suits'!

Suits you, sir

At the end of the 18th century, *men in America started to wear a version of the frock-coat that had a short, or bob, tail. Known as the bob coat, it was the first garment to resemble the modern suit jacket.*

Lounging about

By 1860, some men were wearing a three-piece suit made up of a lounging jacket, matching waistcoat and trousers. The loose cut of the jacket was very different to the snug-fitting frock-coat or morning coat. Their informality made lounge suits very popular with artists, bohemians and intellectuals.

By the beginning of the 20th century the lounge suit had become the accepted informal suit, especially among the young and fashionable. Accessories became more relaxed too, with felt Homburg-hats replacing the traditional black silk topper.

Frock-coat

These stuffy and restrictive formal frock-coats (1839) would soon give way to lounge suits.

Comic dandies

Like many new fashions, lounge suits were considered too outlandish at first. In this cartoon of 1869, the two men wearing modern, loose-cut suits are made to appear rather ridiculous!

Relaxed royalty

The Prince of Wales, later Edward VIII, holidaying with friends. In their light lounge suits and Homburg-hats, they look far more relaxed than the gentleman in the stiff, formal frock-coat.

Lounge suits for one & all

By the 1920s it was acceptable for professional men to wear lounge suits to work, while others wore them to church on Sundays. Lounge suits are still worn, but details such as the width of the lapels, trouser-style, or even the thickness of the shoulder pad, have adapted to changing fashions.

*D*OUBLE-BREASTED SUIT

This still is from the gangster movie, Public Enemy (1931). Double-breasted jackets had become popular during the 1920s.

*S*AFARI SUIT

Lightweight safari suits have long been worn in hot climates. Here Roger Moore, as James Bond, wears a flared-leg version (1978).

*D*RESSED FOR THE CITY

By 1960, suits and ties were standard for the office. Accessories included a trilby or bowler hat – and a brolly, of course!

COATS NOT ONLY PROVIDE EXTRA WARMTH, they also give protection from the rain. In 1823, the chemist Charles Macintosh (1766–1843) patented a wool and India rubber fabric – the first man-made waterproof fabric.

Early raincoats

Macintosh's company sold the first rubber macintoshes, or raincoats. In the 1850s, new rainproofing methods were used for the coats made by Aquascutum (founded in 1851) and Thomas Burberry (1835–1926).

Arctic anoraks

The earliest-known weatherproof coats were hooded, seal-gut anoraks. Worn by the Inuit, they repelled water and snow.

The greatcoat

The greatcoat first appeared in the 1700s. This loose, long-sleeved coat had overlapping shoulder capes to help keep the clothes underneath dry. The style was popular with dandies and coachmen alike. Horse-riders had a special version with a back slit. Both styles are still worn today.

Coats in the trenches

Not everyone fighting in World War I wore a trench coat. This French soldier wears a greatcoat, which was much plainer in style.

PARKAS

Parkas were popular with mods in the 1960s and came back into fashion in the 1990s. Windproof, they have satin lining and large, fur-trimmed hoods.

Trench coats

In the 19th century a military style overcoat with epaulettes first made its appearance. In World War I, a weatherproof version of this was issued to British soldiers. After the war, it was adapted for everyday wear. Trench coats are still worn today and have barely changed. Made in wool or gabardine, they have epaulettes, wide lapels and are belted at the waist.

TRENCH RAINCOATS

In the Pink Panther *films, Peter Sellers (1925–80) was Inspector Clouseau, a bumbling detective. He always wore a classic, trench-style raincoat.*

SKINHEAD STYLE

Crombie coats are popular with skinheads. The overcoats take their name from the cloth they are made from. Crombie is a soft, thick woollen fabric that is made in Aberdeenshire.

TWO KINDS OF ANORAK...

Trainspotters need good waterproofs – that's why they are sometimes nicknamed 'anoraks'!

23

Jeans & denim

IN THE 1850S LEVI STRAUSS (1829–1902) BEGAN SELLING RIVETED DENIM JEANS, *which he called 'waist overalls', to Californian gold prospectors. Denim is a thick cotton fabric that was originally woven in Nîmes, France – its name comes from the French,* de Nîmes *(from Nîmes). In the 1850s, denim was practically unknown; today, it is highly fashionable.*

Anti-fashion for rebels

Westerns of the 1930s had starred cowboys in jeans, but the garment really took off around 1950. Rebellious teenagers adopted workwear because it was cheap and tough. Besides Levi's, Wrangler and Lee were also big sellers. Jeans were worn by bikers, musicians and film stars, notably Elvis Presley (1935–77), Marlon Brando (b.1924) and James Dean (1931–55).

The mark of the individual

By the late 1960s, everyone was wearing jeans. Young people began to customize theirs – hippies sewed on paisley patches, or painted on flowers, while civil rights activists added badges that advertised their cause. A decade later, punks distressed jeans with rips and zips.

Denim haute couture

Denim had been used in the late 1930s by the American designer Claire McCardell (1905–58)

for sporty playsuits. In the late 1970s Perry Ellis (1940–86), Calvin Klein (*b.*1942) and Gloria Vanderbilt (*b.*1924) began to design jeans that were smart – and expensive. Pierre Cardin (*b.*1922), Ralph Lauren (*b.*1939) and Giorgio Armani (*b.*1934) soon added jeans to their collections. Pressed jeans, with Lycra for a better fit, were even worn by Diana, Princess of Wales (1961–97). Today, denim is mainstream fashion worn by young, middle-aged and old alike in both figure-hugging and relaxed styles.

*21*st-century jeans

Madonna reinvented the cowboy look wearing a relaxed, checked shirt and jeans for the video of her song Don't Tell Me *(2000).*

Designer jeans

These jeans by Armani have a leather patch on the waistband. It is a copy of the one used on original Levi's.

Shorts

IN THE FIRST HALF OF THE 20TH CENTURY, *both men and women started to wear shorts for sport and as casual wear. From the 1920s, they were also the standard trousers for young boys, whatever the weather. In Britain, they remain a part of some school uniforms.*

AUSTRIAN PEASANT IN LEDERHOSEN, 1889

Hard-wearing leather shorts, or lederhosen, had been popular in countries such as Germany, Austria and Switzerland for centuries. They were held up by braces.

Short trousers

At the beginning of the 20th century it became fashionable for men to wear shorts when visiting warmer climates. White Bermuda shorts (shorts that reach the knee) are still worn in the tropics by sailors. Lord Baden Powell (1857–1941), founder of the World Scout Movement, made gabardine khaki shorts part of the boy scout uniform.

In the 1930s, there were attempts to replace trousers with shorts. There was even a brief craze for satin evening shorts, but the idea never really caught on! Today, shorts remain popular with boys and men – but only when the weather is warm.

DESERT SHORTS

This still is from Ice Cold in Alex *(1958). The film is set in North Africa during World War II. The heroes wear usual, hot-climate attire – gabardine shorts.*

FIFTIES SHORTS

Shorts became popular with young women in the 1950s. This pair is modelled by French actress, Nicole Maurey (b.1925).

Shorter & shorter

In the 1950s, young women wore short, figure-hugging cotton shorts as casual wear. The look was an instant hit because it showed off the legs to great advantage!

In the early 1970s, hot pants came in. These were the shortest shorts ever, often worn with long socks or high boots to draw even more attention to the legs.

In the 1970s and 1980s tailored shorts were sometimes teamed with jackets for work, but shorts remain an item of casual clothing.

Multi-purpose

These trousers are ideal for unpredictable climates. If the Sun comes out, the legs zip off for instant shorts!

Hot pants

These super-short shorts were very fashionable in the early 1970s. Denim hot pants were home-made, using cut-off old jeans. The frayed, unfinished hem did not matter – it added to the style!

Lycra

In the late 1980s, Lycra was added to cycling shorts. The tight fit reduces air resistance, allowing higher speeds.

Fashionable technology

UNTIL THE MID-19TH CENTURY, TROUSERS WERE PULL-ONS, *held up with braces. Then, tailors developed the fly front, which concealed a row of buttons. Trousers could fit more tightly at the waist and belts began to replace braces. Button-flies remained popular until the 1930s when zip fasteners came in.*

Today's trousers

The zip is still the preferred fastening for trousers. However, some jeans use the old button-fly and appeal to customers in search of a retro look. Braces, too, still have their place in fashion. The trousers of modern dress-suits have waistband buttons for attaching braces, which these days are made using up-to-date stretchy Lycra.

The zip

The original zip, patented in 1893, was large and bulky. It took several decades to produce a zip that was light enough to be used in clothes.

Absolutely riveting!

Copper rivets were first put on jeans in 1873. They stop the seams of bulging pockets from stretching.

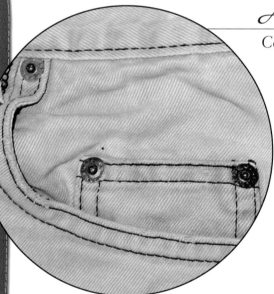

Non-rip material

Torn trousers are a thing of the past with the latest, tough sports fabrics. These shorts are made from non-rip fabric. It is made up of tiny squares, rather than threads, so a rip cannot spread.

Fabrics for the great outdoors

The quest for weatherproof coats and jackets began when Macintosh patented his rubber mix for raincoats in the 1800s. The first waterproofs kept off the rain but were also heavy, smelled bad when wet, and did not allow body moisture to escape.

Today's designers use a range of light, weatherproof fabrics. Polartec fleece was introduced in 1981 and is still being improved – Polartec Power Shield (2002) is wind and water-resistant. Gore-Tex™, which was patented in the 1970s, remains one of the best waterproof fabrics, popular for ski suits and other sportswear. And in labs around the world scientists are creating the next generation of hi-tech fabrics.

How Gore-Tex™ works

The special feature of Gore-Tex™ is a waterproof skin covered in billions of tiny holes, or pores. No rain can penetrate, because each pore is 20,000 times smaller than a raindrop. However, the pores are also 700 times bigger than a molecule of sweat. This means that moisture can evaporate easily through the fabric. The wearer can be as active as he or she likes, whatever the weather, without getting damp from rain – or sweat!

Waterproof

Windproof

Outer shell

Micro-porous, breathable 'skin'

Body moisture escapes

Inner lining

Timeline

Prehistory
The first garment for the lower half of the body was the loincloth.

The ancient world
The ancient Egyptians took the loincloth and passed it through the legs to produce an early trouser-like garment.

The Middle Ages
The Celts and Saxons had worn trouser-like garments called braies, but by CE 1200 they were concealed under the long tunic. A cloak called a mantle gave extra protection against the elements. In the 1400s men wore both long and short tunics and stockings (hose) covered the legs. The mantle developed into a fitted, semicircular cloak called a cope, that draped over the shoulders. The clergy wore decorative copes.

16th century
In the early 1500s, men wore padded doublets over their shirts. These were sometimes slashed to display the white undershirt. The upper half of the hose developed into the 'trunk' which looked like puffed-out shorts and which, like the doublet, was padded. Over the doublet a loose, unfitted jerkin was worn. Jerkins fell to just above the knee. Some had full sleeves, others were sleeveless. Towards the end of the century, the jerkin was replaced by a short, full cloak.

17th century
Men's trunks grew longer and became knee breeches. A full version, known as petticoat breeches, became popular and was often trimmed with lace. Doublets became longer and looser.

18th century
Breeches became narrow and were now worn with waistcoats and knee-length jackets that had wide sleeves. The greatcoat was the most fashionable outerwear for men. At the end of the century men's clothes became less showy, although fine silks and brocades were still worn at court. The square-fronted frock-coat with tails and short-tailed bob coat were introduced.

19th century
Trousers replaced knee breeches. The morning coat became the most popular formal day jacket whilst the frock-coat was incorporated into evening wear. In the 1850s a number of radical ladies started wearing the bloomer suit – a relatively short dress worn with Turkish trousers. The lounge suit was worn by men from the 1860s as informal day wear; for evening wear, the dinner jacket or tuxedo was introduced in the 1880s. In the 1870s Levi Strauss took out a patent on his denim trousers, later to be known as jeans.

20th century & beyond
By the 1920s, women were wearing trousers, especially for sports. Clothing for both sexes became more casual and men adopted sports jackets. Men's trousers had turn-ups and were wider – the widest were known as Oxford bags. In the 1950s, suits with tight drainpipe trousers became fashionable. Jeans were worn by both sexes. In the 1970s flares became popular. At the end of the decade, the punk movement gave birth to an aggressive, scruffy look. Since the 1980s, many styles of coat and trouser have co-existed. Suit jackets in the 1980s had big, padded shoulders to project a powerful image. Youth styles have ranged from outsize skate trousers to the distressed, anti-fashion look known as grunge. Cosy sports clothes are now popular with just about everyone. Jackets and leggings in man-made materials such as fleecy Polartec, weatherproof Gore-Tex™ and stretchy Lycra are an important part of everyone's everyday wardrobe. Padded waistcoats, or gilets, are often worn for extra warmth. And more than a century on, denim jeans remain the most popular trouser of all.

Glossary

G

Braces
The British term for the straps that hold up trousers; Americans call them suspenders.

Braies
Garment worn under a man's tunic to cover the legs. These evolved into drawers.

Brocade
A fabric, often silk, with a raised pattern.

Crinoline
Wide skirts worn from the 1850s, which were supported on a frame of stiff hoops.

Double-breasted
Describes a coat or jacket that has a double line of buttons at the opening at the front.

Fair Isle
A colourful, geometric design, originating from the Shetland Islands, Scotland.

Gabardine
A dense fabric that has a fine diagonal rib effect, popular for suits, coats and shorts.

Gore-Tex™
A man-made, breathable fabric used for weatherproof jackets and trousers.

Greatcoat
A generously-cut outdoor overcoat.

Instep trousers
Trousers with straps that go over the shoe.

Lapels
The front part of the jacket that turns back on itself, above the buttons.

Lycra
A very stretchy man-made fabric.

Morning coat
Plain, dark coats for formal occasions. They have long tails, and the front of the coat slopes toward the tails below waist level.

Single-breasted
Describes a coat or jacket that has a single line of buttons at the opening at the front.

Tails
Back part of a coat that extends beyond the waist, often as far as the back of the knee.

Trilby hat
A soft, felt hat with a dented crown.

Turn-ups
Trousers with the bottom hem pressed up.

Tweed
A coarse, wool cloth woven into a pattern, popular for coats and suits.

Index